C000142546

Spygame

A comedy-thriller

Bettine Manktelow

Samuel French — London
www.samuelfrench-london.co.uk

© 2009 BY BETTINE WALTERS

Rights of Performance by Amateurs are controlled by Samuel French Ltd, 52 Fitzroy Street, London WIT 5JR, and they, or their authorized agents, issue licences to amateurs on payment of a fee. **It is an infringement of the Copyright to give any performance or public reading of the play before the fee has been paid and the licence issued.**
The Royalty Fee indicated below is subject to contract and subject to variation at the sole discretion of Samuel French Ltd.

        Basic fee for each and every
          performance by amateurs   Code L
        in the British Isles

The publication of this play does not imply that it is necessarily available for performance by amateurs or professionals, either in the British Isles or Overseas. Amateurs and professionals considering a production are strongly advised in their own interests to apply to the appropriate agents for written consent before starting rehearsals or booking a theatre or hall.

ISBN 978 0 573 11424 3

The right of Bettine Walters writing under the name
Bettine Manktelow to be identified as author
of this work has been asserted in accordance with
Section 77 of the Copyright, Designs and Patents Act 1988

Please see page iv for further copyright information

SPYGAME

First presented by The New Deal Theatre Company on
Thursday 17th July 2008 at The Gulbenkian Theatre,
Canterbury with the following cast:

Sadie	Pat Hoddinott
Daphne	Deborah Higson
Claire	Claire Woodruff
Steve	George Hannah
Lloyd	Jeremy Anderson
Marie	Joscinda Higginson
Daniel	Brian Bamford

COPYRIGHT INFORMATION

(See also page ii)

This play is fully protected under the Copyright Laws of the British Commonwealth of Nations, the United States of America and all countries of the Berne and Universal Copyright Conventions.

All rights including Stage, Motion Picture, Radio, Television, Public Reading, and Translation into Foreign Languages, are strictly reserved.

No part of this publication may lawfully be reproduced in ANY form or by any means — photocopying, typescript, recording (including video-recording), manuscript, electronic, mechanical, or otherwise—or be transmitted or stored in a retrieval system, without prior permission.

Licences for amateur performances are issued subject to the understanding that it shall be made clear in all advertising matter that the audience will witness an amateur performance; that the names of the authors of the plays shall be included on all programmes; and that the integrity of the authors' work will be preserved.

The Royalty Fee is subject to contract and subject to variation at the sole discretion of Samuel French Ltd.

In theatres or halls seating four hundred or more the fee will be subject to negotiation.

In territories overseas the fee quoted above may not apply. A fee will be quoted on application to our local authorized agent, or if there is no such agent, on application to Samuel French Ltd, London.

VIDEO-RECORDING OF AMATEUR PRODUCTIONS

Please note that the copyright laws governing video-recording are extremely complex and that it should not be assumed that any play may be video-recorded for whatever purpose without first obtaining the permission of the appropriate agents. The fact that a play is published by Samuel French Ltd does not indicate that video rights are available or that Samuel French Ltd controls such rights.

CHARACTERS

Steve
Claire
Lloyd
Marie
Daphne
Sadie
Major Daniels

SYNOPSIS OF SCENES

The action of the play takes place in the lounge of a country house

Time: The present

ACT I
SCENE 1 Late afternoon
SCENE 2 Later in the day
SCENE 3 That night, after lights-out

ACT II The next morning

CHARACTER DESCRIPTIONS

Steve is middle-aged, self-opinionated, pompous, snobbish and self-assured. A man who should have succeeded better than he has, since he had every advantage in life, from education through to choice of career. He knows he is a failure but cannot work out why.

Claire is an amiable, smartly turned out, intelligent, 40-something, but with the arrogance of a woman who is attractive and knows it. She is adventurous and longs for excitement in her life. She works in something glamorous, such as advertising, and at one time fancied she could be a model or actress.

Lloyd is a middle-aged itinerant actor. Contemptuous of authority, Lloyd loves variety in his life. Married once, but his wife couldn't stand the uncertainty of his lifestyle. Irrepressibly good-natured and optimistic he grates on people like Daphne and Steve.

Marie is a youngish housekeeper, with a false middle-European accent. She appears to be Romanian but in fact is not. She is an integral part of the plot and manages to retain her inscrutability in front of everyone except Dan until the end of the play.

Daphne is middle-aged, prim, dowdy and self-possessed. She lives alone, has never married. It is out of character for her to come on something like this but the invitation came at a time when she was feeling particularly low and alone. She is tough and not intimidated by any of the others. She is either a retired teacher or civil servant. She writes poetry as a hobby.

Sadie is middle-aged, slightly older than Daphne, dowdy and rather silly. Naïve, nervous and ingratiating. She tries so hard to please she irritates people. She is a sad, lonely and rather pathetic person, with no children and, until recently, had a domineering husband who managed to reduce what small confidence she had in the first place.

Major Daniels (Dan) is a bright and boisterous, smug, bossy, military man, a background which has influenced him throughout his life. He likes law and order and things done properly. He also enjoys power and is without scruples in using it.

Other plays by Bettine Manktelow
published by Samuel French Ltd

Charity Begins...
Curtain Call
Curtain Up On Murder
Death Walked In
Murder Weekend
Proscenophobia
They Call It Murder
The White Cliffs

ACT I

SCENE 1

The scene is a lounge of a country house. C is an archway. DR is an exit to the kitchen. UL are french windows with curtains and a standard lamp. There is a table on the right with two upright chairs. On the table is a selection of board games. Two upright chairs are either side of the archway, with a small table on the left of it. On the small table, there is a plant pot. There is an armchair R and upright chair DR, settee L and a picture of a country scene with horses on the wall L

Daphne is sitting in the armchair, Sadie is in the upright chair DR. She appears to be nervous. Steve is sitting on the settee with Claire. Steve is middle-aged, smartly dressed, wearing spectacles and reading a broadsheet newspaper. Claire is good looking, casual and smart. She looks bored. Nobody speaks. They are carefully avoiding eye contact with one another. After a while Steve coughs. The others look at him

Steve Excuse me! (*He rustles his newspaper*)

Sadie nods and smiles. The others do not respond. They sit as before with the only sound being Steve turning the pages of his newspaper. After a while Steve clears his throat and the women all look at him as if he is going to speak but he doesn't. Claire reaches in her handbag and takes out her cigarettes

(*Glaring at her over his newspaper*) No smoking.
Claire (*embarrassed*) Sorry! (*She puts away the cigarettes and closes her handbag*)

After another pause, there are noises off C and Marie enters with Lloyd. Marie is dressed very severely in black, her hair scraped back. Lloyd is in casual clothes and untidy. He is boisterous and super-confident

Lloyd Hi!

They all look at him but do not speak. Claire smiles

Marie Pliss! Not to speak! To read!

She hands him a small notice on cardboard. Lloyd reads it and laughs

Not to laugh! Pliss — phone (*She holds out her hand*)
Lloyd Phone?
Marie Pliss! (*She indicates holding a mobile phone*)
Lloyd Why?
Marie Pliss!

Lloyd looks round at the others. They all look away. He hands over his phone

   Marie goes out

Lloyd comes straight DS *and looks around*

Lloyd What a dump!

Sadie coughs nervously and looks at Daphne

Oh, have I said the wrong thing? I suppose one of you doesn't own this palatial residence?
Daphne (*firmly*) We're not supposed to speak.
Lloyd That's a load of nonsense!
Sadie (*nervously*) It was on the card the girl showed you, wasn't it?
Lloyd Yes, but it's stupid. That's what made me laugh. I didn't think it was meant to be taken seriously.
Sadie There must be a reason for it.
Lloyd Then why not tell us? Why the secrecy?
Steve (*rustling his paper and looking over the top of it*) I should think that was obvious.
Lloyd Would you?
Steve If you're here for the same reason as we are it is obvious. Unless of course you happen to be a delivery man.
Lloyd No, I'm not a delivery man, but I suppose I could be anything! But whoever I am I don't intend to be told when I can and cannot speak.
Steve Rules were meant to be broken, is that it?
Lloyd As far as I'm concerned, yes. We're not children. Why should we be told not to speak?
Claire (*relaxing*) I thought it was silly too!
Lloyd Good — there's one free spirit amongst you. I'm Lloyd. (*He goes over to Claire*)
Claire Claire—Smith.

They shake hands

Daphne (*severely*) We're not supposed to use our real names.

Claire I'm not.

Lloyd Neither am I.

Sadie (*disappointed*) I was going to call myself Smith.

Claire It doesn't matter. We can both be Smiths.

Steve We can't all be Smiths.

Lloyd I don't see why we can't all be Smiths. We're going to be together for a few days. We'll be like one big happy family. I'm Lloyd—Smith.

Sadie (*rather enjoying the game*) I'm Sadie Smith, no relation!

Lloyd That's right! (*Pointing to Steve*) And who are you?

Steve I don't know who gave you the right to put yourself in charge?

Lloyd Somebody has got to do something! How would you answer an interrogator? You wouldn't say "I don't know who gave you the right to put yourself in charge", would you?

Steve (*stuffily*) That is hardly the case.

Lloyd (*formally addressing him*) Name, rank and serial number!

Steve We're not in the army.

Lloyd We're being recruited, aren't we?

Steve Not for the army.

Lloyd A kind of army, a pretend army. I still think the rules apply. As we haven't a rank or serial number we should at least be sure of our names.

Steve (*peeved*) All right! Steve — Smyth — with a "y".

Lloyd Great! As long as we're not captured together we should be all right.

Sadie (*alarmed*) We're not going to be captured, are we?

Lloyd Who knows? We could be taken hostage. They might like to know how we'd react in a hostage situation.

Sadie Oh, I do hope not!

Daphne (*giving a little cough*) You forgot to ask my name.

Lloyd So sorry! What do you call yourself?

Daphne Daphne — Doubleday.

Lloyd Oh, not a Smith! Good! Daphne Doubleday.

They shake hands

I love alliteration!

Sadie (*surprised*) Do you?

Lloyd Phew! That took some sorting out. If we're like that about everything we're not going to learn much in five days!

Steve (*severely*) We really shouldn't be talking at all, should we?

Claire Looks like we are though, doesn't it?

Daphne Now we've broken the ice!

Pause

Sadie It's funny, isn't it? Now we've started talking we don't know what to say.

Lloyd I expect it's all part of the test.

Sadie Do you think so?

Lloyd Oh yes — they've probably got hidden cameras and microphones all over the place and they're listening in to see how we get on. (*He looks around the room with shrewd interest*)

Sadie (*nervously*) I do hope not!

Claire If that is the case why would they tell us not to talk?

Lloyd I expect that's part of the test too. Just to see which one of us would break the rules.

Steve That seems rather childish!

Lloyd I suppose the whole thing is rather childish! But it should be fun.

Claire And it is a free holiday.

Sadie Do you think it will be a holiday?

Claire Of course — a free holiday, all expenses paid. If you're bored stiff and got nothing to do what better way to spend a few days?

Sadie I just liked the idea of being on television. I love reality shows. I thought how wonderful actually to be on a reality show. That's what it will be like, won't it, for whoever wins out of us? One of us will be a star!

Lloyd Yeah, that's right! Whoever wins goes on the live show! On the other hand they could be taping us now to go out live, just like Big Brother, only we're the dimwits who don't know about it.

Steve (*brusquely*) They couldn't do that!

Lloyd Why not?

Steve A gross infringement of privacy.

Lloyd But they could do it. We all gave our consent.

Sadie Did we?

Lloyd We all signed a contract, didn't we?

Sadie I do remember signing something, but I couldn't read the small print.

Lloyd You should always read the small print.

Steve You wouldn't be here unless you'd signed the contract. I assure you I read it. There was nothing about filming us until the actual show goes out. What we were signing was to absolve them from any responsibility should anything go wrong.

Lloyd That's right. Like when you go into hospital, in case you die of MRSA.

Sadie We're not to going to die, are we?

Claire That's not what he meant!

Lloyd Isn't it?

Claire I think you're a bit of an alarmist.

Lloyd Am I?

Daphne The main thing everyone seems to have forgotten is that we are not supposed to be speaking.

Sadie Yes, that's right. I suppose they're afraid we'll let something slip. (*Looking round nervously*) We mustn't tell one another our real names or circumstances. That was in the contract.

Lloyd You read that bit then?

Sadie It was only the small print I couldn't read.

Daphne The bit about the false alibis was in big print. They were adamant about that. We mustn't let anyone know where we were really going. We had to make up a false alibi. I must say I did wonder about that. Why all the secrecy?

Sadie It seemed fun to me, having to pretend to be going somewhere we weren't going and not telling anyone the truth. I like secrets.

Lloyd You'll make a good spy then.

Sadie (*pleased*) Oh! Will I? Thank you.

Claire I thought up quite a good alibi. I told them at work I had to do jury service and I didn't know how long it would take and I couldn't be in touch with anyone until the trial was over. They were all impressed.

Lloyd When you go back they'll want to know all about it.

Claire I shall say it was too boring to repeat!

Lloyd (*with a speculative look at her*) I don't think it will be boring!

Claire We don't know yet, do we?

Lloyd So — any more alibis? (*Addressing Sadie*) What about you?

Sadie (*rather taken aback*) Oh me! I just told the neighbours I was going on holiday. I said I didn't know where. It was one of those surprise holidays.

Lloyd Very good! Not a lie, because I'm sure it will be a surprise!

Daphne I told my friend I was going into retreat.

Sadie I wouldn't have thought of that? (*Pause*) What is retreat?

Daphne It's where you go to contemplate spiritual matters.

Sadie I suppose that's why I've never heard of it. I'm Church of England.

Lloyd (*to Steve*) So what was your cover story?

Steve An assignment in the Middle East. I'm a journalist.

Lloyd Oh, that's good! If you don't come back nobody will bother to look for you!

Steve There's no earthly reason why I shouldn't come back.

Lloyd Just joking!

Claire (*to Lloyd*) What about you?

Lloyd I'm an actor, so people are used to me disappearing for a few weeks now and then. I said I was making a film in the Andes.

Claire Why did you choose the Andes?

Lloyd It had to be somewhere remote and I don't know anyone who's been there, so they couldn't ask me about it when I got back. So that's the lot of us! I reckon we've been quite imaginative.

Pause

Daphne I was just thinking, listening to you, that we must all live alone.
Sadie Why did you think that?
Daphne Because nobody mentioned having to make an excuse to a wife or husband or anyone.
Lloyd That's right! Are we all loners, so to speak?

They all look at one another and murmur agreement

Claire I wonder why we were picked.
Daphne What makes you think we were picked?
Lloyd Many are called but few are chosen!
Daphne I hope you are not mocking me.
Lloyd What on earth makes you think that?
Claire I wonder how many people they contacted.
Sadie I didn't think I stood a chance. I'm so surprised to be here.
Steve (*with a disparaging look*) They did say the most unlikely people would be chosen.
Lloyd I suppose you all saw it on the internet?
Steve No, I received an email. It intrigued me. I can't resist a challenge.
Lloyd Answering a random email! You should have known better.
Steve I couldn't see the harm. They were not asking for my bank account details, or for that matter any personal details. It seemed *bona fide*. I'm not stupid.
Lloyd And there was the lure of easy money, quite a lot of money for the winner, in fact.
Steve Oh, it wasn't the money. I'm not interested in the money.
Lloyd Of course not.
Claire I received an email too. I wondered whether to answer it, but it sounded like an adventure. What about you?
Lloyd Just the same! To an out-of-work actor anything is a distraction, and there again, I do need the money. (*Looking at Daphne and Sadie*) What about you? How did you know about this thing?
Sadie I haven't got a computer. A very nice man rang me up and said how would I like to be on television. I watch television all the time and I thought how thrilling to actually be on television. He told me it was a random sample. I'd never been a random sample before. I couldn't resist it.
Lloyd (*to Daphne*) And you?
Daphne I was also contacted by phone. It was someone very polite and persuasive.
Lloyd Obviously! So that's the lot of us! I wonder how many others have been chosen for this event.

Claire Do you mean the competition?

Lloyd Exactly, and what is the criterion?

Sadie What do you mean?

Lloyd Why were we chosen?

Steve I suppose they wanted to attract as wide a cross section as possible to draw us into their net.

Lloyd I do feel a bit as if I've been "hooked".

Daphne They didn't say which channel, did they?

Claire No, I thought that was odd.

Sadie I thought it must be the BBC. The man on the phone was ever so polite.

Lloyd Pompous and patronizing? That sounds like the BBC.

Sadie Oh no, he was ever so chummy and friendly. He made me feel quite special.

Lloyd In that case it's probably Channel Five. (*He crosses* L)

Steve I sincerely hope not!

Lloyd (*reaching up and peering into a picture on the wall*) How strange! This very nice picture has a hole in it.

Lloyd takes it down. There is a hole in the wall. He turns to the others triumphantly

Stand by for action, folks — you're on Candid Camera!

Sadie What do you mean?

Lloyd There's a camera, love, behind the wall.

Daphne That shouldn't be allowed.

Steve I told you we should be quiet!

Lloyd Yeah, OK, mate, you can go to the top of the class.

Dan enters

Dan Good! You found it! Great! I wondered how long it would take you. Record time, in fact, one of the best, no pun intended! I'm Major Daniels. I'm in charge. No need to introduce yourselves. I know who you are. In fact, I'm the only one who does know who you are. That makes for security all round. You were right, Lloyd — everything is a test, from the minute you come in until you eventually leave. We will tell you at the end how you got on, your marks, so to speak

Lloyd What's the competition like?

Dan Quite steady! We had thousands of contacts but we whittled them down to two hundred. The final six will appear in our "How to Be" series on a new BBC channel next year.

Sadie So it was the BBC?

Dan Of course. Who knows, you could even be a star!

Sadie (*thrilled*) A star! Oh, how marvellous! You mean like on Big Brother?

Dan Something like that. Although I think you're probably all too intelligent to be taken to the heart of the general public. They love stupid people! They make them feel so clever. On the other hand if you appear too stupid in any of our tests you will not be picked, so you pays your money and you takes your choice, although in this case we pay the money, not you! It's public money so there's plenty of it. Now then you will be glad to know that you have all passed the first test.

Sadie But we all spoke when we were told not to.

Dan Ah, but you were encouraged into that by Lloyd. Before that you did as you were told. The English are notoriously good at not talking to strangers but I felt sure one of you would disobey the rules, and once that happened you all followed suit. That too bears out my philosophy. People only need a leader to break the rules.

Steve I don't agree. I do not think that someone who breaks the rules is a leader. He is a rebel. I for one would not follow a rebel.

Dan Many rebels become leaders. It happens all the time. However, we won't discuss that right now. We are not looking for leaders, but followers.

Lloyd Where do I fit in there?

Dan You all have a part to play. Let me explain. You have been singled out as the most likely candidates for our programme on "How to be a Spy". The five days you spend here will be to see if you could convince the television audience that you are the real thing, because when the show goes out we will have some genuine spooks taking part. It is up to the audience to guess which are which, or who is who or whatever the case may be and then phone in with their votes. We are expecting a big response. It's audience participation which is what the public love.

Lloyd And it's a great source of revenue.

Dan I won't deny it. But that isn't the reason behind it.

Lloyd Isn't it?

Dan Of course not. We don't need that sort of revenue. We leave that to the commercial channels! Now then, I'm going to ask you a few simple questions just to get you relaxed.

Lloyd I am relaxed.

Dan You first then. Does the idea of being a spy appeal to you?

Lloyd Yes, very much.

Dan Could you tell me why.

Lloyd I'd like to kill somebody.

Dan Just anybody, or somebody in particular?

Lloyd No one in particular.

Dan I see. (*Turning to Claire*) What about you?

Claire I don't want to kill anybody.

Dan So what attracts you to the idea?

Claire It sounds like fun!

Dan Exactly! Good answer! (*To Sadie*) And you?

Sadie I've always wanted to be on television. I was so thrilled to be asked. I thought I could be famous!

Dan You never know! Stranger things have happened! (*To Daphne*) And you? Why did you agree to take part in this little venture?

Daphne Curiosity — and boredom.

Dan Good enough! (*To Steve*) And you, sir?

Steve It's a challenge. I'm the sort of person who needs constant challenge.

Dan Well said! OK, so I think I've got the picture. We will start training tomorrow in the art of deception. Women are usually the best at that.

Daphne That's a sexist remark!

Dan I beg your pardon. It was meant to be a compliment. Now then, your luggage has been taken up to the rooms allocated to you. The housekeeper will show you where they are. Oh, by the way, don't try to engage her in conversation. She speaks hardly any English. That's why we chose her.

Sadie I knew she was a foreigner.

Dan We try to avoid using the word "foreigner" at the Beeb. It might offend someone.

Lloyd Only the foreigners!

Dan (*glaring at Lloyd*) Marie is simply a visitor helping us out with this assignment.

Sadie Like an exchange visit? Is she here to learn the language?

Dan Not exactly, since she is not supposed to speak to you.

Lloyd Except to remind us not to speak!

Dan Exactly!

Lloyd Does she understand what we say?

Dan Only a little.

Lloyd So we must be on our guard.

Dan You should always be on your guard.

Lloyd Where is Marie from?

Dan Romania. Have you been there?

Lloyd 'Fraid not!

Dan Good! That's enough about Marie! Now then, you must not expect luxury here. There are quite extensive grounds and you can wander around at will, but you must not go outside the gates. There are no phones and no computers. Alcohol and smoking are not permitted. That's the rule. Breakfast is served at o-eight-hundred hours. Thereafter there will be training and testing. Lunch is at thirteen-hundred and supper sharp at nineteen-hundred hours. Lights out is twenty-two-hundred hours. This is run like a military establishment. That means punctuality, respect and obedience to the rules.

Lloyd That might prove a bit difficult.

Dan It aims to be. You have some time to yourselves now before supper.

Lloyd (*glancing at his watch*) What, half an hour? You're spoiling us!

Claire I take it we may speak to one another during that half an hour?

Dan You may.

Sadie That's good! I love finding out about different people.

Dan You should still be careful what you say. You are not to divulge your true identity.

Sadie That's the hard part!

Dan Before you disperse I have to tell you that tomorrow you will all undergo a rigorous medical examination.

Steve Why is that necessary?

Dan We don't want any of you to die on us, do we?

Daphne Why should any of us die?

Lloyd I hope you're not subjecting us to physical jerks!

Dan Not at all!

Sadie I couldn't stand up to torture! I thought I'd tell you that now.

Dan There's no question of that. I would remind you that it is all pretend. Nothing more than a game, but we still need to know that you're fit. There may be a few shocks along the way. We are as interested in your mental state as much as your physical. Those of you who can endure mental stress will be the most likely winners.

Lloyd That lets me out!

Dan (*with a hard look at Lloyd*) Now — a quick test of your observation. Shut your eyes!

Lloyd Why?

Dan Shut your eyes! All of you!

They shut their eyes

Now then, (*going up to Daphne and putting his hand on her shoulder*) Daphne — how many steps up to the front door?

Daphne (*thinking carefully*) There were — three steps up to the front door.

Dan Capital! (*Addressing Sadie*) Sadie, what colour is the carpet in this room?

Sadie Oh dear! I'm not sure. I think it's red or is it green, or is it a mixture? I'm sure it's a mixture. Yes, a mixture of red and green.

Dan Humph! Now then, Claire — on the wall behind you is a picture. What does it depict?

Claire (*thinking hard*) It's a — a country scene, I think. Yes, a country scene.

Dan Not bad! Steve — can you improve on that?

Steve There are horses. It's a well-known print.

Dan Excellent. You may all open your eyes.

Sadie Oh good! Well I wasn't completely wrong about the carpet.

Lloyd What about me? You didn't ask me anything?

Dan I'm about to. On the wall facing you as you entered the house there was a plaque. Can you remember the inscription thereon?

Lloyd (*with a disparaging look*) Abandon hope all ye who enter here!

Dan (*triumphantly*) You can't remember?

Lloyd What about "*Honi soit qui mal y pense*"?

Dan (*disappointed*) Well — yes, that's right.

Lloyd Sorry!

Marie appears in the doorway

Marie Zee rooms are ready!

They all look at her

(*Looking ahead stonily*) Pliss — to come!

She turns smartly round and goes out

Lloyd I can't believe that girl! Why can't she smile? Has she been programmed?

Dan She's simply following orders — (*aiming this remark at Lloyd*) which I hope you will all do.

Lloyd What's the accommodation like? Are we sharing?

Dan Absolutely not. Nor should there be any visiting between rooms.

Lloyd None at all?

Dan None! You are all here to learn, not to socialize!

Lloyd (*glumly*) I see.

Dan Now then — Marie is waiting for you!

They all get up and begin to make their way to exit C. There is murmured conversation, overlapping one another as they speak

Claire What a weird set-up!

Lloyd This is just the beginning.

Daphne I'm glad we can't go into one another's rooms. I need to have my quiet time.

Sadie Oh, I hate having quiet times!

Dan (*above the other voices*) Oh, by the way. By the way!

They stop to look at him

A word of advice! I told you to be on your guard and that is for a very good reason. One of you is a mole!

They all look at one another suspiciously

Black-out

Scene 2

The same. Later in the day

The Lights come up on an empty stage

Lloyd is the first to enter, followed by Claire. Sadie is trying to join in the conversation, Daphne is behind her and Steve brings up the rear

Steve goes straight across to the french windows and looks out. Lloyd and Claire stand c. Sadie puts her handbag on the armchair and joins them, hovering by Lloyd's side. Daphne goes to sit in the armchair, seeing Sadie's handbag she sits in the upright chair DR

Lloyd I had filled in every single thing on the form. I said I could fence, ride a horse, etc. and I couldn't do anything like that, so when they told me the next scene was on horseback I nearly had a fit!

Claire What did you do?

Lloyd I took the job. I thought it can't be that difficult to ride a horse, but when I vaulted on the bloody thing I just fell straight off!

Claire Oh dear! (*She hides a smile*)

Sadie How awful!

Lloyd (*ignoring Sadie*) I broke my ankle and that was the end of my career as a film extra!

Sadie I've never done anything like that. I'd be too scared!

Claire You have had an interesting life!

Lloyd Yes, I suppose I have. (*Ignoring Sadie and speaking to Claire*) But I never could take orders, you see. I had to be an actor or a journalist or doing something freelance. I can't bear being told what to do.

Claire But actors are told what to do, aren't they?

Lloyd Well, to a certain extent. You have to do as the director tells you but that's only in the beginning. Once you're at the top you can please yourself. The trouble was I never got to the top.

Sadie Just because you fell off a horse! That doesn't seem fair.

Lloyd (*still ignoring Sadie and speaking to Claire*) Now then, you tell me about yourself?

Claire (*modestly*) Oh, there isn't much to tell. (*She moves to the settee*)
Lloyd (*following her*) I'm sure there is. For instance, are you now or have you ever been a member of the married fraternity?

They both sit on the settee. Sadie hovers behind them, sees there is nowhere to sit and, looking downcast, goes over to the armchair and sits. She looks at Daphne, but Daphne is reading a magazine and ignores her

Claire No, and I don't want to be.
Lloyd Great! Neither do I!
Steve (*stuffily*) Isn't this touching? (*Behind Lloyd over the back of the settee*) We're supposed to be here to learn how to be spies, not to chat one another up!
Daphne (*looking up briefly from her magazine*) I quite agree.
Lloyd (*rising to speak to him*) How do you know this isn't part of it?
Steve I can't see how!
Lloyd We have to form relationships, don't we, in order to worm secrets out of people?
Steve That isn't my interpretation of spying, I assure you! Mata Hari seducing the enemy and exchanging pillow talk — that's a bit old-fashioned, isn't it?
Sadie What do you mean?
Lloyd (*ignoring Sadie and addressing Steve*) Whatever! I think you'd be miscast as a gigolo!

Claire smothers a laugh

Steve I shouldn't want to be, I assure you!

Marie enters from kitchen DR with five cups of coffee, sugar bowl and milk on a tray

Marie Pliss — coffee ist here! (*She takes the tray of coffee round during the following dialogue, firstly to Daphne and Sadie, then to Claire and Steve, lastly to Lloyd*)
Sadie Thank you. Coffee always finishes a meal off nicely, doesn't it? Can I help you?
Marie Pliss to sit down. All! (*She looks round at them all, frowning*)

Steve sits next to Claire on the settee. Lloyd glares at him

Lloyd I'd rather stand.
Marie Pliss?

Lloyd Oh, all right. (*He sits on the upright chair* LC *against the wall*)
Sadie (*politely*) It was a nice meal, wasn't it?
Lloyd If you like that sort of thing.
Sadie (*to Marie*) Do you do the cooking?

Marie ignores her and goes on taking round coffee

Claire She doesn't understand you.
Lloyd She doesn't want to, you mean! It wasn't exactly a nice meal!
Sadie (*defensively*) It was all right!
Daphne It depends what you're used to.
Lloyd Too right!

Marie has reached Lloyd

I don't drink coffee.
Marie Pliss to drink somesing.
Lloyd Somesing?
Marie Pliss!
Claire You're offending her. She feels rejected.
Lloyd Oh dear, we can't have that, can we? (*He takes a cup of coffee*)
Steve (*irritably*) I don't know what she's doing here. Why couldn't they get
    someone who can speak English?
Sadie They don't want her to tell us anything.
Steve That's all very well, but we can't tell her anything either.
Marie Pliss?
Lloyd He said thank you for the coffee.

Marie looks at Lloyd puzzled and shakes her head

  Merci! Danke schön!

Marie still looks puzzled

Marie Pliss to drink! (*She motions drinking*)

They obediently appear to drink

  Marie nods, smiles and goes off R

Lloyd Disgusting stuff! (*He tips his coffee in to the plant pot on the table next
    to his chair*) I prefer my own nightcap.
Sadie Nightcap?

Lloyd A drop of the hard stuff.

Steve No alcohol!

Lloyd Get stuffed!

Steve You are no gentleman.

Lloyd I don't aspire to be.

Claire Oh, come on. Don't let's fall out. We have to get on.

Lloyd Why?

Daphne Squabbling won't help. We have to be together for a few days. We should be able to co-exist. We're all adults.

Lloyd Yes, you're right. I'm sorry! (*Standing up and looking thoughtfully at the picture* L) Though it could be that they want us to fall out. They could be watching all the time.

Sadie That's a bit creepy — being spied on.

Lloyd The spies are spied on! We should get used to it.

Claire You were right about the coffee. It's diabolical! (*She goes over and tips her coffee in the plant pot*)

Lloyd Good! You can join me in a nightcap later on!

Claire I'm not sure that's a good idea.

Steve It's a bad idea. He said no alcohol. You'll get into trouble if he finds out.

Lloyd I think they probably want us to get into trouble, don't you? Everything that happens here is a test.

Sadie You mean — we shouldn't do as we're told?

Lloyd I mean they are looking for individuals. Work out for yourself what that means.

Sadie looks puzzled. There is a pause

Daphne I think we should bear in mind that there is supposed to be a mole amongst us.

Sadie Oh yes—

Lloyd Don't look at me!

Claire If it was you, you'd be bound to deny it.

Steve It's too obvious that it's him.

Lloyd Perhaps it's meant to be too obvious!

Sadie I'm not going to think about it. What does it matter whether there's a mole or not?

Steve It could be a test. Find the mole or we're not selected.

Claire He didn't say that, did he?

Lloyd All he did was give us instructions. I must say I didn't think they'd treat us like a load of monkeys.

Sadie Monkeys? (*She rises in alarm*)

Lloyd They're experimenting with us, aren't they? I just wish they'd get on with it.

Steve Get on with what?

Lloyd The tests — the training — whatever it is!

Daphne It will all start tomorrow.

Lloyd So what do we do tonight?

Sadie (*going to the table* R *and putting down her coffee cup*) It does seem funny without television.

Steve It's a relief!

Sadie (*at the table*) There are some games here. That'll pass the time.

Lloyd Let's have a look — Monopoly — that takes too long. Cluedo! Ludo! Oh, give it rest. Scrabble!

Sadie I love Scrabble! I'm not very good at it though.

Lloyd Right. We'll play Scrabble. Who else?

Claire I don't mind.

Daphne I'd rather not. You can come and sit here. I'll move.

Claire Thanks.

Lloyd and Sadie sit at the table R*. Claire takes Daphne's chair and also sits at the table. Daphne goes across to Steve and sits next to him*

The Lights dim R *and a spot concentrates on* L

Daphne I'm no good at parlour games.

Steve Neither am I. They bore me.

Daphne I'm quite happy with my own company.

Steve So am I!

Daphne Oh, sorry. I didn't know where else to sit.

Steve No — I didn't mean right now. Sit here by all means. I'm sorry. I'm afraid I've forgotten my manners these days. Not used to feminine company, you see.

Daphne What are you used to? Oh, I suppose we're not supposed to ask that. No personal questions.

Steve That's what the man said. But I've nothing to hide. I've lived most of my life abroad. My father was in the diplomatic service and I followed suit.

Daphne You have all the right attributes to be a spy then.

Steve Not really. We don't go in for spying at our embassies. We leave that to the others.

Daphne Oh, I didn't mean that.

Steve The worse thing for my parents was coming home. My mother had lived abroad so long she'd forgotten how to cook if she ever knew! She spent years just socializing. After a while I think she forgot who she really was. Her personality disappeared into a morass of platitudes and gracious behaviour. She was always a lady. She just wasn't a woman.

Daphne That's rather judgemental, don't you think?

Steve Yes, it is.

Daphne Were you the only son?

Steve Oh yes, the only everything! Quite a burden! I tried to make the grade in the diplomatic corps but I hadn't my father's temperament. I don't suffer fools gladly!

Daphne Neither do I.

Steve What I would have liked to do is simply be a beach bum and wander round the Caribbean playing piano in bars and drinking all night! Trouble was I couldn't play the piano.

Daphne I think you're a frustrated adventurer.

Steve Yes, I suppose I am. That's why I'm here. (*Pause*) It's odd, here we are, practically strangers and I'm telling you things I haven't said for years — haven't thought about for years either! Odd that, isn't it?

Daphne Perhaps the fact that we were told not to confide in one another has made us more keen to confide. Do you think that could be the reason?

Steve I don't know. That fellow over there spent the whole of dinner talking about himself, but I should think he always does.

Daphne That's my impression too!

Steve What about you?

Daphne What?

Steve Do you mind talking about yourself?

Daphne (*reluctantly*) I'm not used to talking but I'm not used to listening either. Sometimes I don't say a word to anybody all day. I haven't even a cat or dog to talk to. I'm allergic to animal fur.

Steve You must be lonely.

Daphne No, I'm not. I actually resent people intruding into my life. I hardly exchange a word with anyone in the shops. What's the point? I just get on with my shopping and go home. I'm happy when I close the door against the world and can be alone again. That's what I like.

Steve Don't you go to work or anything? Oh, there I go, asking personal questions.

Daphne I don't mind telling you. I work from home. I'm a poet.

Steve How interesting! "Shall I compare thee to a summer's day..." that sort of thing?

Daphne Not quite. I write verses for greetings cards,

Steve (*heartily*) Oh, good for you! I often wondered who wrote that stuff, I mean, those words.

Daphne (*tersely*) A lot of people buy greetings cards. They read a lot into the words. You'd be surprised!

Steve I'm sure you're right. I'll bet they're jolly good. I shall think of you the next time I buy one.

Daphne Thank you.

Steve You are a dark horse! I would never have taken you for a poet!

Daphne So, what would you have taken me for?

Steve Just nice and ordinary, I suppose. Oh, sorry is that too blunt?

Daphne Not at all. I like people to think I'm ordinary.

Lights comes up R when there is a shout of laughter from Lloyd

Lloyd That's it! I'm out! I've won!

Claire (*protesting*) You wouldn't find that word in the dictionary! (*She points*)

Lloyd Of course, you would! Just not the same dictionary! Well, that's that! Doesn't time fly when you're having fun!

Sadie I said I wasn't very good at it. (*Going across to the others*) May I join you?

Steve Yes, you can sit here. (*He rises from the settee*)

Sadie I don't want to turn you out.

Steve That's all right. We've had our little chat. Did you know this good lady was a poet?

Daphne (*annoyed*) Please don't tell everyone!

Steve I thought you'd be proud of it.

Daphne I am in a way. I just don't want to talk about it.

Sadie Heavens, a poet! Are you famous?

Daphne (*crossly*) Not at all, not at all famous.

Sadie I would love to be famous. I've never done anything to make me famous. I mean I've never done anything good enough.

Steve You could always do something bad enough. Like Jack the Ripper for instance. Everyone remembers him. If you can't be famous you could be infamous.

Sadie (*alarmed*) Oh why did you say that? That's different. I wouldn't like that at all! You shouldn't say things like that!

Steve I didn't mean to be taken literally... (*He gives her a derisory look and goes up to the french windows and looks out*)

Sadie (*turning to Daphne*) Oh dear, that's a habit of mine, taking things literally. My husband used to say that. I never knew when he was joking. He was always saying funny things——

Daphne (*interrupting her*) Yes, quite! (*She pointedly turns her back and takes out a little book of poetry from her handbag and begins to read*)

Sadie looks suitably rebuffed

The Light fades on them L and a spot comes up on Claire and Lloyd R. They move DS

Lloyd So we have the medical to face tomorrow and the interrogation! That should be fun.

Claire What will it be like — the interrogation?

Lloyd I think they'll expect us to lie and see if we can do it cleverly. Perhaps we should have a dummy run?

Claire A what?

Lloyd Try it out! I'll ask you a few things and then you can ask me.

Claire OK.

Lloyd Now, the things they trap you on are factual. For instance — age and date of birth!

Claire Oh no, you don't get me on that one.

Lloyd If you make something up you must remember it, that's all.

Claire I'm no good at figures. I'd never remember it.

Lloyd All right! Here's another one. Where were you born?

Claire South — Southampton.

Lloyd Why aren't you married?

Claire That's personal.

Lloyd There's nothing personal about being a spy. Make something up.

Claire I was married.

Lloyd Ah, that's better. What happened?

Claire He wanted the things I didn't want.

Lloyd Such as?

Claire Children.

Lloyd So why didn't you want children?

Claire They disrupt your life.

Lloyd You must have had an unhappy childhood.

Claire No, I didn't. I had a happy childhood. My father was a vicar——

Lloyd Don't volunteer too much! Why tell them things they don't need to know? If you're making it up it just gives you more to remember. Just keep to the facts.

Claire OK, start again!

Lloyd Where were you born?

Claire South London.

Lloyd You said Southampton.

Claire Did I?

Lloyd Caught you out! So are you married?

Claire Not now.

Lloyd What happened?

Claire My husband ran away with my twin sister.

Lloyd An identical twin?

Claire Yes.

Lloyd He changed the person but not the woman.

Claire In a sense yes.

Lloyd What was the difference between you?

Claire She wanted children.
Lloyd I see. (*Pause*) How much of this is true?
Claire None of it.
Lloyd I don't know whether to believe you or not.
Claire Good! Now my turn. Are you the mole?
Lloyd No!
Claire Why do you want to kill someone?
Lloyd To find out what it's like.
Claire Do you want to experience everything in life?
Lloyd Yes, everything I can.
Claire Why aren't you married?
Lloyd I was.
Claire What happened?
Lloyd She disappeared.
Claire Now we go into the realm of fantasy!
Lloyd No, it's true. The police thought I'd killed her.
Claire And did you?
Lloyd I told you. I haven't killed anyone — yet.
Claire (*laughing*) My God! You can shoot a line! How much of that was
true?
Lloyd All of it!
Claire Oh — I've had enough of this. I really must have a smoke!
Lloyd Let's go outside.
Claire OK!

The Lights come up as Dan comes to the archway

Dan How are you all enjoying yourselves?
Lloyd Marvellous. Thanks!
Claire We were just going outside.
Dan You can't do that. It's lights out. Twenty-two-hundred and you have a
busy day ahead of you.

*Lloyd and Claire look disgruntled. Lloyd shakes his head to her not to
say anything*

It's just as well to retire now. Remember we want you up bright and breezy
in the morning for your medicals. Once that's over we will get down to
serious business.
Lloyd Learning how to be a spy!
Claire That will be fun!
Dan You know the way to your rooms so off you go!
Steve Just like prep school being sent to bed by the housemaster!

Dan Yes, it is like that! Discipline and obedience. There are no radios and the lights will be off at the mains in half an hour, so no reading in bed. There are small battery lights at your bedside but otherwise the house is in darkness, so no stumbling around in the corridors or you might get hurt.

Sadie Heavens! I wouldn't leave my room in a strange house whatever happened. (*She crosses* R *to pick up her handbag from the armchair*)

Lloyd I suppose you haven't got an attic with a raving lunatic locked up. Shades of Grace Poole!

Dan I assure you, there's nothing to be afraid of. It's just that we want to be sure you all do as you're told. Now then, I'll just stay here to put out the lights after you. Goodnight to you all!

They file out rather sheepishly muttering goodnight to each other

Lloyd is the last to leave

Lloyd Aren't you going to tuck us in?
Dan I'll leave that job to Marie.
Lloyd Don't bother!

Lloyd goes off

Dan stands looking round the room. He goes over and switches off the standard lamp UL *and draws the curtains at the french windows*

Marie enters from kitchen with a tray

Marie (*without an accent*) I thought they'd never go. (*She goes round collecting coffee cups as they talk*)
Dan You put something in their coffee, I take it?
Marie Of course, and they drank it.
Dan They should be feeling sleepy by now.
Marie Pity we haven't got a few younger ones, spice it up a bit.
Dan We did have a few but they had too much baggage.
Marie Baggage?
Dan Yes, you know what I mean, doting mothers, fond fathers, inquisitive lovers, just too much baggage!
Marie Oh yes, that wouldn't do, would it? (*At the table* R) It looks as if they played Scrabble. I thought Snakes and Ladders would be more their style!
Dan Good job they didn't start Monopoly. (*Ominously*) They won't be here long enough to finish that.
Marie I hope not. I do wish you hadn't saddled me with this foreign accent. It's such a struggle to keep it up.
Dan Don't worry, you're doing OK. It's better for you to pretend not to

understand them than to have to answer all their silly questions. They'd soon
trip you up.

Marie Am I that stupid?

Dan That's not what I mean, but you're not as devious as I am. You'd give
the game away.

Marie (*indignantly*) I wouldn't give the game away! What do you take me
for?

Dan Calm down! You wouldn't mean to but you couldn't help it if they all
started having a go at you, quizzing you. Believe me, I know what I'm talking
about. Let's just leave things the way they are.

Marie I don't have much choice, do I? It would be highly suspicious if I
dropped my accent now.

Dan Then you must be sure you don't. You should always be on your guard
— as I've told them.

Marie (*wearily*) OK, I get the message. Is everything ready?

Dan Oh yes, *alles in ordnung!* Come on then, lights out!

They go out through the kitchen DR. Dan turns off the light by the door

Black-out

SCENE 3

The same. That night after lights out

Dim Lighting comes up on Lloyd sitting on the settee with an unlit torch

*Claire enters cautiously, flashing a torch around. She goes over to the wall L and
puts her hand underneath the picture*

Lloyd I've already done that.

Claire (*with a gasp*) Oh, I didn't see you there.

Lloyd (*flashing his torch at her and then on himself*) I've put something over
the hole. A bit of soap, actually, so whoever looks out will get a sore eye.

Claire Good idea! I've been sitting on my windowsill having a smoke and
waiting for the others to go to sleep. It was really peaceful. I could hear an
owl hooting.

Lloyd I wasn't sure if you'd heard my whispered message on the staircase.
Our secret assignation!

Claire I couldn't reply, could I, not with Sadie right behind me?

Lloyd I wasn't sure you'd come.

Claire We'll have to be careful, won't we? The whole place could be
bugged.

Lloyd We'll have to take that chance. (*Crossing to the french windows*) I'm going to pull back the curtains — there's a full moon. We can't keep flashing our torches about. (*He pulls back the curtains*)

Moonlight streams in

There—that's better.

Claire It's a lovely spot, isn't it? A velvety sky!

Lloyd No industrial smog. We can see the stars. Quite romantic!

Claire It could be with the right person. Why did you want to see me?

They turn off their torches and sit on the settee. Dim spotlight on them

Lloyd Just an idea I had. We have to beat them at their own game.

Claire How?

Lloyd Look at it like this. They are trying to trip us up all the time but if we form an alliance, you and me, they can't do it. They're betting we'll turn against one another, be competitive. That's why they chose such disparate people.

Claire Did you say disparate?

Lloyd Yeah — not desperate. But the point is if we form a little partnership we can help one another. You back me and vice versa.

Claire I see. Why did you pick me?

Lloyd Please!

Claire You mean the others are hopeless.

Lloyd What do you think?

Claire As long as you haven't an ulterior motive.

Lloyd (*innocently*) I don't know what you mean.

Claire OK! So how do we beat them at their own game?

Lloyd They're encouraging us to tell lies, to deceive one another, to see how good we are at it, so we should make a pact not to tell lies to one another, only to the others.

Claire And you think that will work?

Lloyd It gives us a sporting chance.

Claire As long as we trust one another.

Lloyd Listen, I was a boy scout. My word is my bond.

Claire All right!

They shake hands on it

Lloyd (*holding on to her hand*) I meant that about a nightcap. You're welcome to come up to my room and accept my hospitality.

Claire I'll think about it.

Lloyd OK, no rush! It's cosy sitting here in the dark, isn't it? There's something about the dark that makes one wax confidential. (*Giving her a sidelong glance*) It reminds me of the time I spent at boarding school.

Claire Whereabouts?

Lloyd Oh, you'd never have heard of it — in the wilds of Kent. We used to sneak away on a summer's night and sit outside a country pub. Then we'd send the biggest boy inside to order six pints of cider. Nobody queried it.

Claire Always the rebel — even then!

Lloyd (*nostalgically*) We were all rebels in our own way, our little crowd. I well remember those fine summer evenings, we'd sit there until the sun went down, and the crickets would start their night chorus and we'd be feeling all mellow and happy in a sad kind of way. We all knew that youth was passing and nothing would ever be the same again. It was an unspoken thought that passed between us, a nostalgia for something that was fading but hadn't quite left! Sad!

Claire I wouldn't have placed you as a public school boy.

Lloyd Who said anything about public school?

Claire But you said you were a boarder.

Lloyd It was a reform school.

Claire (*rising; cross at being taken-in*) Oh you! I thought you said we were going to be honest with one another.

Lloyd I am being honest. I didn't say it was public school. You just assumed it. Now it's your turn. (*Rising and facing her*) What was all that nonsense about your husband running off with your twin sister?

Claire But it was true. He did.

Lloyd An identical twin.

Claire Absolutely! We had to wear different coloured hair ribbons at school for anyone to tell us apart.

Lloyd I'm going to give you a tip.

Claire What about?

Lloyd Being interrogated. You have to be very careful about your body language. It will give you away.

Claire Are you saying I have given myself away?

Lloyd You weren't telling the exact truth, I know that.

Claire How do you know?

Lloyd I watched your eyes — they kept shifting from right to left, the right is the memory and the left is the creative side, so your eyes go to the right when you're telling the truth and the left when you're lying — or could it be the other way round? Anyway, it gives you away.

Claire So what's the answer? What's the "tip"?

Lloyd When you're being interrogated look straight ahead.

Claire That's easy!

Lloyd It's easy when you're telling the truth, but not when you're lying. You have to practise.

Claire So have you practised?

Lloyd Some!

Claire Let me ask you something then.

Lloyd OK!

Claire Look at me!

Lloyd looks at Claire

What happened to your wife?

Lloyd She wasn't actually my wife.

Claire Whatever she was — what happened to her?

Lloyd I told you she disappeared. The police thought I'd killed her.

Claire You promised to tell the truth.

Lloyd I am! I've never killed anyone.

Claire But she really disappeared?

Lloyd Yes, without a trace.

Claire It's strange, if you're telling the truth that we both have someone in our background who has disappeared.

Lloyd Your husband didn't disappear, did he? You said he'd run away with your twin sister.

Claire So he did, but they disappeared. I've never heard from either of them again, and neither has anyone else I know.

Lloyd You're a quick learner. I noticed you looked at me all the time you were telling me that.

Claire (*sitting on the settee*) Do you think I was lying?

Lloyd (*sitting beside her*) I don't know. Do you think I was?

Claire We have to believe one another, don't we?

Lloyd It would help. But to test your theory we could ask the others if they have some sort of secret in their background, an inexplicable disappearance from someone in their lives.

Claire That's a good idea.

Lloyd That could be the link between us.

Claire Does there have to be a link between us?

Lloyd I think there must be.

Claire Why?

Lloyd Because we were all contacted personally, weren't we? We didn't volunteer. We didn't see it advertised in the nationals or on the internet. They contacted us.

Claire So you think they chose us?

Lloyd It seems likely, doesn't it? We're all so different. There must be a link.

Claire That makes me nervous. What reason could they have?

Lloyd That's what we have to find out.

A car door slams outside the window

Listen! What's that?
Claire A car?
Lloyd At this time of night? (*He gets up and creeps across to the french windows and looks out cautiously*)
Claire What is it?
Lloyd Shush! (*He stands in front of the window, blocking her view*)
Claire Was it a car?
Lloyd No, a hearse!
Claire Are you sure? A hearse! (*Staring out front*) What can it mean?

Black-out

ACT II

The same. The next morning

Sadie is sitting on the settee looking rather dismal. Claire enters from the archway

Sadie Oh, I'm so glad you've come in! I wondered where you'd gone after the medical.

Claire I just went for a walk. It's such a lovely day.

Sadie Did you see Daphne? I don't know where she is. She wasn't at breakfast.

Claire No, I didn't see anyone. Did you pass the medical? (*She sits next to Sadie on the settee*)

Sadie Oh yes, did you?

Claire Yes, quite easily. Of course I didn't tell them I smoked.

Sadie Oh, why not?

Claire (*with a pained look*) What do you think?

Sadie I suppose that would go against you. I'm sorry, I'm not thinking straight. I'm worried about Daphne.

Claire Why?

Sadie She wasn't at breakfast and I heard her crying last night. Her room is next to mine. I'm sure I heard someone crying. It was quite pitiful!

Claire (*mischievously*) It might not have been her. It could have been a ghost!

Sadie (*scared*) Why do you say that? You don't really think that, do you?

Claire Only kidding!

Sadie That's good! I'm easily scared. I can't help it. I'm rather a nervous type and I woke up feeling uneasy today. I get these feelings sometimes.

Claire I suppose everyone does.

Sadie I hope so. I hate to think I'm different.

Claire I like to be different. (*Wandering over to the french windows*) I've had a nice walk this morning. There are very extensive grounds here with iron railings all the way round. I went as far as the front gate. It was locked.

Sadie You didn't see Daphne, I suppose? Oh no, you said you didn't.

Claire I didn't see anyone. It was a bit strange, though, not only was the gate locked but there was a large dog prowling around by the side of it.

Sadie Outside or inside?

Claire Inside, of course. It was tethered to a post near the gate. What I mean is you couldn't get through the gate without facing it.

Sadie What sort of dog was it?

Claire A big black one.

Sadie I shan't go and look. I'm afraid of big black dogs.

Claire I suppose if they're going to have a guard dog it's no good having a Pekinese.

Sadie Daphne told me she's allergic to dogs.

Claire I can't see why they need a guard dog. It's not as if we're going to run away! Why should we?

Sadie I expect it's to keep people out.

Claire What people?

Sadie I don't know. (*Looking at the picture*) Do you think——?

Claire Are they listening? I don't know.

Sadie (*going up to the wall; addressing the picture*) If they are listening I'd like them to know I was disappointed by the breakfast. I like a proper breakfast when I'm staying somewhere. I don't call croissants a proper breakfast. I like an English breakfast, bacon and egg and all the trimmings.

Claire Not healthy though, is it? All that fat!

Sadie It's never done me any harm.

Claire (*doubtfully*) No? Has Lloyd gone in for his medical? Do you know?

Sadie I think so. I don't really know what's going on.

Claire I went out to see if there was a village shop nearby and I could get a newspaper. I hate not knowing what's going on in the world.

Sadie I didn't see a village when we drove here, let alone a village shop. It was just countryside.

Claire We didn't approach through a village but there might have been one in the opposite direction. Anyway, I knew I couldn't get past that dog, even if the gate had been unlocked. They do seem to be very security conscious. (*She looks hard at the picture*)

Sadie It's nice to feel secure.

Claire Is it? How secure are we?

Sadie What do you mean? We are secure, aren't we, in here?

Claire I'm not sure. I don't know if we can trust them.

Sadie Trust who? You mean the Major? You are making me nervous.

Claire I didn't mean to.

Sadie Why shouldn't we trust them?

Claire It's just a feeling I have.

Sadie I have a feeling too, a feeling about Daphne. I read somewhere that you should take notice of these feelings, you know, intuition. We ignore them, but often they do mean that something's wrong.

Claire But why should something be wrong with Daphne?

Sadie I don't know. I wish I knew where she was. I was talking to her last night when you were talking to Lloyd. She's rather a sad person, lonely, like me. I suppose that's why we came on something like this.

Claire I'm not lonely. I'm very busy. I have a very full life.

Sadie I didn't mean you — sorry! I meant Daphne and me. It's nice to be busy. I used to be busy.

Claire What happened?

Sadie I went into a depression. It was after my husband left.

Claire That's what they call a life-changing event.

Sadie It certainly changed mine.

Claire Did he tell you why he left?

Sadie He said he wanted to find himself. I didn't know he was lost.

Claire And is he lost now?

Sadie What do you mean?

Claire Did he disappear?

Sadie Disappear? (*Alarmed; standing up*) Why did you say that?

Claire (*moving* R; *thinking about it*) It's just something we were talking about last night, Lloyd and I. It's just a theory. We wondered if there was a link between us all, the people who are here, and we wondered whether that link could be a mystery in our past, like somebody disappearing.

Sadie (*dismayed*) A mystery? What do you mean?

Lloyd enters. He goes over to Claire

Lloyd What a joke!

Claire Was it?

Lloyd Not half. The medical! PULHEEMS!

Claire PULHEEMS?

Lloyd The medical. PULHEEMS! That's what they call it in the Mob.

Sadie In the Mob? (*Horrified*) Do you mean the Mafia?

Lloyd No, no, the Mob is the Forces, the armed services, that's what the Mob means to an Englishman. PULHEEMS stands for pulse, urine, lungs, heart, ears, eyes, muscles and something else I can't remember.

Sadie So that's what they were doing, checking up on things like that.

Lloyd That's it! Passed with flying colours despite the fact that I drink, smoke and please myself about life. Never exercise! I hate exercise. Thoroughly, delightfully, unhealthily fit! That's me!

Steve enters looking pleased

(*To Steve*) OK?

Steve I passed A-one!

Lloyd Oh good! So did I.

Steve (*disappointed*) Are you sure?

Lloyd Of course, I'm sure.

Claire So it looks as if we all passed! That's good!

Steve So, what happens next? I'm raring to go. Love a challenge! (*He moves to the french windows*)

Lloyd I've got a feeling you might get one!

Dan enters

Dan I'm pleased to say that you all passed your medical with flying colours.

Lloyd Nice to know we're all fit for whatever you're going to put us through.

Sadie (*going to Dan*) But what about Daphne? Where is she?

Dan I was about to add all except the lady you know as Daphne. I'm afraid she didn't pass her medical. She is going home.

Sadie (*to Claire*) There — you see! I knew something was wrong.

Dan Nothing is wrong. We just can't take chances on people. We must make sure you're up to it before we start our training.

Lloyd Up to what?

Dan Anything.

Sadie Poor Daphne. She will be disappointed. I must say goodbye.

Dan Too late. (*Looking out of the french windows*) She's just leaving now. There's no point in hanging about. We sent for a taxi.

Sadie Where is she? I can't see her. (*Trying to pass Dan to go to the french windows; calling out*) Daphne! Daphne! Oh, there she is!

Dan (*firmly standing between Sadie and the french windows*) Please keep away from the window.

Sadie But I'd like to say goodbye.

Steve So would I.

Dan Better not — she was rather upset.

Sadie Oh dear, I am sorry. Poor Daphne!

Steve stares through the window during the following

Dan Never mind. In a way it's easier having two couples. Now, this morning I am giving you the opportunity to see interrogation techniques at work. I will take two of you into the study and interrogate one while the other watches to see what mistakes you make, and then I will take the other two. You two first. (*Pointing to Steve and Sadie*) You others stay here.

Lloyd OK by me!

Sadie Oh dear, why do we have to go first?

Steve Get it over with.

Dan Come on — you'll enjoy it!

Dan, Steve and Sadie exit

Lloyd What do you make of that?

Claire What?

Lloyd Them sending Daphne home.

Claire I don't know. Listen, I wanted to tell you something. I've just been for a walk. I went right down to the gate.

Lloyd I saw you through the window. It's not much of a garden.

Claire It's not a garden at all, just a plot of land with a few trees and iron railings all round with a gate at the end of the drive, a locked gate.

Lloyd I'd expected that.

Claire But there was something else, at the gate.

Lloyd Well?

Claire A guard dog. A Doberman, I should think, just sitting there glowering at me. I didn't attempt to go near. (*Glancing at the picture*) Is it all right to talk?

Lloyd Don't worry about that! They haven't unblocked the hole. I came down before breakfast and had a look.

Claire Oh good! But what do you make of it all? What are they playing at?

Lloyd Are they keeping intruders out or keeping us in?

Claire What do you think? And what about last night?

Lloyd What about last night? Did I miss something?

Claire Outside the window! Did you really see a hearse?

Lloyd Ah yes, that did give me a jolt, but thinking about it this morning, I thought I must have made a mistake. It could just have been a black taxi.

Claire You seemed sure about it last night.

Lloyd Yes but I only had a glimpse of it. I thought they'd see us looking out of the window.

Claire Who would see us?

Lloyd Well, anybody. But it couldn't have been a hearse. I mean— nobody's dead, are they?

Claire No, of course not. (*Pause*) But why did they want a taxi anyway? It was after lights out. It does seem odd. I wish we'd stayed to see what happened.

Lloyd What do you mean — what happened?

Claire Who got out of it?

Lloyd Or in it.

Claire In it? If it was a taxi you mean? I was thinking about that when I went to bed. I couldn't sleep. I tried to lock my door but the lock didn't work.

Lloyd Neither did mine. Funny, isn't it?

Claire I put a chair against it. I didn't want anyone making a mistake about their room.

Lloyd (*innocently*) Who on earth would do that?

Claire You never know! I can't understand why they expect us to be so fit. It's not as if we're going to be real spies and have to survive the third degree.

Lloyd It was all a bit over the top, wasn't it, the so-called medical? All that jumping up and down before taking our blood pressure. What were they getting at?

Claire And what about the blood test? We're not here a week. It always takes ages to get a blood test result on the NHS.

Lloyd P'raps they've got their own laboratory.

Claire Oh, really! Their own laboratory! This is for a TV programme, not real life! Why would they have their own laboratory?

Lloyd Why take our blood at all for that matter?

Claire Make sure we're not HIV positive, I suppose.

Lloyd But even if we were, how does that affect a TV programme?

Claire I haven't had a blood test for ages. I'd like to know the result.

Lloyd If they start walking around with plastic gloves on you'll know the result!

Claire Oh you!

Steve and Sadie enter looking despondent

Lloyd How was it?

Steve Disappointing.

Dan enters behind them

Dan Right, (*indicating Claire and Lloyd*) next pair. (*Indicating Steve and Sadie*) You two can practise the interrogation technique.

Dan goes out followed by Claire and Lloyd who exchange glances as they go

Sadie (*sitting on the settee*) I don't think I could interrogate anyone.

Steve (*sitting on the chair* R) I don't see why we should, to be honest. Surely they have different people for that?

Sadie I don't know. (*Pause*) Did you really think it was disappointing?

Steve Of course. I thought it would be a battle of wits — him trying to discover things we were trying to hide. But it wasn't like that at all. It was just like going to the doctors. What ails you and here's the prescription. Stand up, speak up and shut up!

Sadie He didn't give you a prescription, did he?

Steve I was speaking metaphorically.

Sadie Oh, I see. (*But she doesn't*) I didn't know what to say to him. I thought if I tell a lie he'll only trip me up. Did you tell him the truth?

Steve Of course not!

Sadie You were very convincing.

Steve (*pleased*) Oh, good!

Sadie All that business about being in the Secret Service, that wasn't true?

Steve Secret Service? Me? Not at all! I thought I'd make it all so implausible he'd know it was a lie, but he didn't seem to suss it out at all. Nowhere near as brilliant as he makes out, that fellow!

Sadie Still, I suppose if you were in the Secret Service you wouldn't tell the truth anyway, would you?

Steve Ah, I see what you mean. A double bluff! Yes, he might have thought it was a double bluff, in which case he isn't quite as stupid as he appears.

Sadie Was any of it true, what you said?

Steve Bits! When he asked me my foibles or faults I admitted that I am a bit obsessional.

Sadie What does that mean, exactly?

Steve I like everything just so! (*Standing* C; *illustrating what he means with his hands*) For instance I must have everything put away tidily in the bathroom, bottles lined up in order of height, the large ones at the end, the smaller ones in the middle. My wife could never get the hang of that.

Sadie Oh, I thought you weren't married.

Steve I'm not now.

Sadie What happened?

Steve It was all about the bed.

Sadie Please don't tell me anything personal.

Steve No, it's all right. You might agree with me. You see, I like the corners tucked in at the end.

Sadie The end?

Steve (*patiently*) The end of the bed. Where I went to school the matron was very keen on beds being neat and tidy, the corners tucked in just so and the sheet turned back. They didn't have duvets, they were for pansies...

Sadie You weren't sleeping in the garden? Oh, sorry!

Steve (*with a glare*) But the same thing applies because my wife always puts a sheet under the duvet.

Sadie Oh yes, so do I! Saves washing the duvet every week.

Steve Quite so! However, my wife never could get the hang of making the corners and it all came to a head one Sunday morning when I went into the bedroom and saw she'd made a real hash of the bed. She hadn't bothered with the corners at all. I didn't exactly fly into a rage but I was cross and told her so and to my amazement she just let out a scream and jumped out of the window.

Sadie (*shocked*) How terrible! Did she die?

Steve No, it was a bungalow. But she hurt her ankle, and she went voluntarily into a psychiatric hospital for a little rest. She never came out.

Sadie Oh, dear, you must miss her!

Steve No, actually I don't!

Sadie Well I never! (*She looks at him aghast*)

Steve Why anyone should think the marital state is the ideal one I don't know!

Sadie So, in a sense your wife disappeared.

Steve She certainly disappeared out of the window. (*Peering out of the french windows*) Well, that's odd!

Sadie What is?

Steve The taxi that took Daphne to the station, it's back again.

Sadie Oh yes? (*Going to look*) How do you know it's the same taxi?

Steve I saw the taxi driver. He has a beard.

Sadie (*quite alarmed*) Oh dear! Do you think someone else is going somewhere?

Steve Perhaps, but the point is when we came here it took us half an hour to get from the station. A taxi could hardly be there and back in less!

Sadie (*puzzled*) No, I suppose not! I just don't understand what's happening. I can't understand Daphne leaving like that, so abruptly.

Steve Neither can I. I thought she had much better manners than to go without a word to anyone.

Sadie I thought that too.

Steve A very nice woman I thought from our brief acquaintance, quite unusual.

Sadie Yes, she was, I mean is, and a poet as well. I've never met a poet before.

Steve Neither have I and I can't believe that anyone who writes poetry would be so bad-mannered as to leave without a word.

Sadie I thought it was odd. I said that to the others, but they didn't take any notice of me.

Steve They wouldn't!

Lloyd and Claire enter, laughing

Lloyd What a waste of time!

Claire You certainly tied him up in knots. He gave up on you.

Steve What happened?

Lloyd I started interrogating him! He didn't like it at all!

Claire And quite abruptly terminated the interview.

Steve Is he still in the study?

Lloyd He walked out.

Steve I want to see him.

Steve exits

Claire (*to Sadie*) When the Major stormed out of the room I could have collapsed! (*Turning to Lloyd*) What do you think he'll do? Send us all home?
Sadie There's something odd going on ...
Lloyd (*ignoring Sadie; answering Claire*) Why should he? He was only cross with me.
Claire No, he was cross with me too, because I laughed. I just couldn't help it. (*She laughs again*)
Sadie I want to tell you...
Lloyd (*ignoring Sadie again*) I suppose it was funny! I was just annoyed!
Sadie (*raising her voice*) Listen to me! *Please!*

They both stop laughing and stare at her

Sadie Sorry! Only there's something wrong.
Lloyd What?
Sadie Steve noticed something. He's gone to see the Major.
Lloyd What about?
Sadie You know we saw Daphne getting into a taxi.
Lloyd I didn't actually see her.
Sadie I did. At least I saw her back.
Claire So?
Sadie The taxi she left in. It's back again.
Claire I can't see the significance. Sorry if I'm dumb.
Lloyd I see what she's getting at. Why should there be a taxi here? Is someone else going somewhere?
Sadie It's not just that. Steve pointed out that it took us half an hour to get from the station yesterday. How could the taxi have driven Daphne to the station and come back here since we saw her leave? There just isn't time.
Lloyd It's a different taxi.
Sadie No, Steve said it was the same driver. He saw him. He has a beard.

Pause. Claire and Lloyd exchange glances

Lloyd Are you sure you saw Daphne get into the taxi?
Sadie I thought it was Daphne. I didn't see her face. If she didn't leave where is she? (*Pause*) You don't think something has happened to her, do you?

Marie enters and addresses Lloyd

Marie Pliss — to come! (*She beckons*)
Lloyd Why?

Marie Pliss — to come now!
Claire What do you want him for?
Marie (*staring at her without expression*) Pliss?
Claire Oh, I forgot you don't understand.
Marie (*pointing to Lloyd*) Pliss to come! (*She turns away*)
Lloyd (*to Marie*) Your slip is showing!

Marie turns round at once and looks at her skirt, then catches Lloyd's eye and glares at him

Marie Oh!

  She dashes off

Lloyd That got her!
Sadie What do you mean?
Lloyd She looked round, didn't she?
Sadie But she can't understand English.
Lloyd Yes, she can.
Sadie Oh dear, I am in a muddle. If she can understand English why is she pretending?
Lloyd It's all part of it — to get us "at it".
Sadie (*wailing*) I don't understand why!

  Dan enters, looking annoyed

Dan I'm afraid you've upset Marie. She didn't know what you were saying but she knew you were making fun of her. It is really not acceptable.
Lloyd Like her pretending not to understand English.
Dan She doesn't understand English.
Lloyd I think she does.
Dan I would like to know your evidence.
Lloyd No doubt, but I'm not telling you. You'll have to bring on the thumbscrews!
Dan These feeble jests are not appreciated!
Lloyd Try another one. Where's Daphne?
Dan She went home.
Lloyd How do we know?
Dan You saw her — out of the window?
Lloyd I didn't see her. All Sadie saw was her back.
Sadie Yes, that's right.
Lloyd It could have been anyone.
Dan But it wasn't anyone. You'll have to take my word for it.

Lloyd Why should we?

Dan glares at him

Claire What was wrong with Daphne, to make her go home?
Dan That is strictly confidential.
Lloyd You can tell me, I promise I won't split. I was a boy scout!
Claire You'll be asking us to sign the Official Secrets Act next!
Lloyd For all we know we did sign it. We signed enough stuff yesterday.
Sadie Oh, heavens! I don't understand what's going on at all. Where's Steve now?
Claire Has he gone home as well?
Dan Funny you should say that.
Lloyd Why?
Dan He is going. He's packing.
Sadie (*dismayed*) Oh no!
Claire I didn't mean it!
Lloyd Why is he going home? He passed the medical.
Dan It's his own wish. He has personal reasons.
Sadie He won't go without saying goodbye, will he? Like Daphne did.
Dan He doesn't wish to see anyone. He has had some bad news.
Lloyd What sort of bad news?
Dan We ask the questions!
Lloyd You've got the wrong accent!

Dan glares at him

Sadie (*tremulously*) I'd like to say goodbye to him.
Dan Well, you can't! He's very upset. He's had some bad news about his wife.
Sadie His wife?
Dan Yes, so please settle down. We'll just continue with the three of you. I should tell you by our present reckoning of observation and interrogation Sadie Smith stands head and shoulders above the rest of you.
Lloyd Oh! And she's only little!
Sadie Me? Oh, heavens, do I?
Dan Certainly.
Claire Clever girl!
Dan Now then we will see how well you all pass the next test.
Lloyd What is the next test?
Dan You'll find out when you least expect it. Just wait and see.

Dan exits

Claire I can't think how you came out top of the class.

Sadie Neither can I! I didn't try.

Lloyd You can't reason it out. For instance, how did anyone get a message to Steve when we are all supposed to be incommunicado?

Sadie Yes, and there are no phones either.

Claire (*sarcastically*) Exactly!

Sadie I don't think Steve would be worried about his wife. He'd just been telling me that he hadn't seen her for years and he didn't want to.

Lloyd I know we're treating this like a bit of fun, but supposing it isn't? Supposing it's deadly serious.

Sadie Don't say that!

Lloyd I've been thinking about it. Daphne goes home or is purported to have gone home and now Steve is going, both without a word to us! Doesn't that seem odd?

Sadie I'm really surprised Daphne didn't say goodbye to me. I thought she liked me.

Claire What are you getting at?

Lloyd Think about it. Everyone of us is a loner. We agreed that before.

Claire That's right!

Lloyd So no one is going to make a fuss if we disappear. It would be easy to make us all disappear, wouldn't it? It would be months before anyone would investigate. By which time there would be no evidence.

Claire Evidence of what?

Lloyd Evidence of our disappearance.

Sadie But why would they want us to disappear?

Lloyd I don't know that yet. (*Pause*) Perhaps they want to steal our identities.

Sadie What for?

Lloyd Get at our money. Use our passports. Just be us! It's always happening.

Sadie Is it?

Lloyd Of course. That's why you should never answer a random email.

Sadie (*wailing*) But I didn't answer an email. They phoned me up.

Lloyd They must have targeted you.

Sadie (*horrified*) Targeted me? But why?

Claire (*not seriously*) I suppose they could be aliens!

Sadie Like that film *The Invasion of the Body Snatchers*. (*She gives a little scream of terror*)

Lloyd and Claire cross to her to shush her

Lloyd (*patiently*) We don't know the reason! Let's not be too fanciful. If they want to get rid of us they must have a reason, a real motive, not sci-fi — real life!

Claire But what she said about body snatchers isn't all that fanciful. Bodies are quite useful now for spare parts.

Lloyd Yes, I suppose you're right there. There are never enough donors for all the dying patients! If I was rich enough I'd buy a spare part to keep on living, wouldn't you?

Claire Even if it meant killing someone to get it?

Lloyd Why not?

Sadie Killing someone! Oh no! (*Collapsing on the settee*) This can't be happening!

Lloyd Nobody said it was happening! We're surmizing.

Sadie Oh, please, don't go on surmising. You're scaring me stiff! I think I'll go home. (*Crossing to Lloyd*) They can't stop me, can they?

Lloyd They might try.

Sadie I'll go and tell them now. I can leave with Steve. He won't mind. (*Going towards the arch*)

Lloyd No — wait! (*Taking her arm and leading her back*) The Major said you were in the lead. You don't want to pass up on winning, do you? Missing the chance of being on television?

Claire And winning lots of money!

Sadie I don't know. I don't think it matters so much now. I'm too frightened. (*She begins to cry*)

Claire (*comforting her*) Don't be frightened. We were just supposing what might happen. There's no reason why any of us couldn't just walk out right now.

Sadie (*calming down*) Isn't there?

A shot rings out. Marie screams offstage. They all start with alarm

What was that?

Lloyd A shot.

Claire It came from the study.

Sadie drops down in a faint behind the settee

Lloyd Look after her!

Lloyd exits c

Claire tries to bring Sadie round. They are both behind the settee

Claire Sadie — you'll be all right. I'm sure it was nothing. Look, I'll get you some water.

A groan from Sadie

Claire exits into the kitchen

Lloyd comes back in with Dan

They come straight DS, so Dan doesn't see Sadie behind the settee

Dan I tell you the bloke went berserk. It's nothing to do with us. Poor Marie had a fit! She nearly passed out I must take her some water.
Lloyd Do you mean he's running around with a gun?
Dan I don't know.
Lloyd Someone better find him before he does some damage.
Dan Well — you go. You're the action man, aren't you?
Lloyd Not in real life I'm not. (*Looking out of the window*) There he is. What is he up to?
Dan Go after him and find out!
Lloyd Oh yeah!
Dan Somebody has to. (*Sinking down on the settee*) I'm not up for it.
Lloyd So much for the military training.

Lloyd exits through the french windows

Marie staggers in C

Marie I thought you were going to get me some water.
Dan I was. It just came over me that I'd had a brush with death!
Marie I don't think he meant to shoot you. (*She sits next to him on the settee*)
Dan He certainly gave that impression.
Marie What on earth was he doing with a revolver?
Dan How should I know? I was as surprised as you were.
Marie This is going beyond a joke. I think we should wrap it up.
Dan What do you mean?
Marie Pack it in. Wrap it up. I don't reckon I'm being paid enough for being shot at.
Dan He wasn't shooting at *you*. How do you think I feel?

Sadie groans from behind settee

Marie What was that? Somebody's there!
Dan (*peering behind the settee*) It's one of them.
Marie What's she doing on the floor?
Dan I don't know. Do something!

Claire enters with a glass of water

Claire Here you are, Sadie! (*Stopping as she sees the others*) Oh!
Dan (*rising and going over to her*) What happened here?
Claire I was about to ask you that.
Dan The poor lady seems to have fainted. Marie will look after her.

Marie glares at him

I won't be a minute.

Dan goes off c

Claire What was that noise just now?
Marie Pliss?
Claire The noise! The shot! Bang! (*She gestures*)

Marie shrugs. Sadie lets out another moan

(*Putting down the glass on table by the settee*) Could you help me get her up?
Marie Pliss?
Claire (*indicating*) Up!

Marie nods. Between them they get Sadie up

Sadie (*mumbling*) Oh dear, what happened? I am a nuisance. Oh dear...
Oh dear...
Claire (*soothingly*) You'll be all right. You fainted, that's all.

They sit her on the settee

(*Giving her the water*) Here you are. You'll feel better in a minute.
Sadie (*coming round*) What was that noise? (*Trying to get up*) Is anybody dead?
Claire Shush, shush! It was nothing.
Sadie What was it?
Claire I don't know exactly but it can't be anything much. Lloyd's gone to look.

Marie glances at her sharply

Marie Excuse pliss!

Marie exits c

Sadie I wish I understood what was going on.
Claire So do I.

Steve enters through the french windows

Oh!
Steve (*whispering*) It's only me. Where are the others?
Claire What others?
Steve Everybody.
Claire (*irritably*) I don't know where everybody is. Don't ask me. What have you been playing at?
Steve I haven't been playing at anything
Sadie Did you hear that gun shot? Has anybody been hurt?
Steve Nobody's been hurt. It was an accident.
Claire It was you. You had a gun?
Steve I didn't know it was loaded.
Claire That's an old excuse.
Steve It's an old song as well, but it happens to be true.
Claire What were you doing with a gun?
Steve Giving him a scare. Trouble was I scared myself as well. Damned nearly shot myself in the foot.
Claire Shot yourself in the foot!
Steve I know it sounds ridiculous. I brought the gun with me as a precaution. I guessed there would be tricks going on. I've watched enough reality shows to know that, so I thought I'd turn the tables on them. That's what spies do, isn't it?
Claire You were just playing the game?
Steve Exactly, and I defy any of you to cap that one.
Claire You want to win?
Steve Of course. I thought we all wanted to win. A hundred grand is not to be sniffed at.
Sadie I don't like guns.
Steve One chamber must have been loaded. I didn't realize that.
Claire Where did you get it?
Steve Something my father always carried around with him. We travelled to some dangerous places in those days.
Claire What did you do with the gun? I mean where is it now?
Steve I don't know. I dropped it.
Claire You dropped it?
Steve I wish you'd stop repeating everything I say.
Claire It's all so implausible! You having a gun, shooting yourself in the foot, dropping it! I'm just surprised the Major hasn't called the police.
Steve I'm not.

Claire You're not?

Steve No, I'm not surprised he hasn't called the police.

Lloyd enters through the french windows

Lloyd I've been looking for you. What are you playing at?

Steve I've just been explaining to Claire. I nearly shot myself in the foot.

Lloyd Shot yourself in the foot!

Clair We've been through all that.

Lloyd What an earth did you want a gun for anyway?

Steve It was a precaution. It wasn't loaded. At least I thought it wasn't loaded.

Lloyd I don't know how you concealed it. I swear someone searched my luggage.

Steve I thought that too. I hid it in my sock.

Lloyd Oh, brilliant! I suppose you saw that in a film.

Steve Actually, I did!

Lloyd Pity you didn't also see in a film how to check a gun before you point it at someone!

Steve I didn't point it at anyone. In fact I was just holding it by my side. It's a long time since I've used a gun.

Lloyd You're telling me!

Steve I assure you in my hey-day this would have been no problem. But I'm out of practice. I think that's why the gun went off. I haven't the same control over my trigger finger.

Lloyd Very nasty that if you can't control your trigger finger.

Steve Why is everything such a big joke to you?

Lloyd Because I think that's what it is — a big joke, everything that's happening here.

Steve Well, you're wrong! And I can prove it.

Lloyd How?

Steve Daphne didn't leave.

Claire She didn't leave?

Sadie (*rising*) Oh, heavens. Where is she?

Steve They're holding her — against her will.

Sadie (*tragically*) Oh no, poor Daphne! Against her will! Oh dear, I knew something was wrong! What are we going to do? (*She collapses back on the settee*)

Steve I'm doing something, don't worry!

He ducks out and exits through the french windows

Lloyd What is the guy up to?

Claire Sadie, are you all right? (*Going to her*) You look awful.

Sadie No. No. I'm all right. I'm just so confused!

Claire It is confusing, but you can trust us.

Sadie I'm not sure I can. I'm not sure I can trust anyone. That girl — that Marie — I heard her speaking English.

Lloyd There, you see, I said so!

Sadie How do I know you're not all pretending?

Claire Why should we be pretending?

Sadie Perhaps you can't help it. You might not be who you seem. Sometimes people look like themselves but underneath they're somebody else.

Lloyd Do you mean like aliens?

Sadie (*moving* DL *in agitation*) Yes, you might look like human beings but inside you're really a lizard or some other reptile.

Claire I don't think so!

Sadie (*with horror*) Or even worse, demons!

Lloyd Come off it — demons!

Sadie (*crossing to Lloyd* C) Yes, a demon can take over someone's body. Any minute your heads will start swivelling round and you'll let out some bad language!

Lloyd The bad language bit wouldn't surprise me at all!

Claire Sadie, I think you're getting too worked up about this.

Sadie No, I'm not. It could happen. I saw something like it on television.

Lloyd I think you watch too much television.

Sadie You can't watch too much television.

Claire Of course you can.

Sadie You just don't like to think I've worked it out, that's all!

Lloyd They said you were top of the class.

Claire So what do you think is going on?

Sadie Can they hear us? (*She looks at the picture on the wall*)

Lloyd I should think they're otherwise occupied at the moment. The Major seems to have completely lost his nerve, if he ever had any!

Sadie That's all an act. He knows!

Lloyd Knows what?

Sadie All about us. (*Significantly*) All about our secrets.

Claire (*puzzled*) What secrets?

Sadie We've all got secrets, haven't we? You said that yourself. Secrets about somebody disappearing in the past.

Lloyd Why did you tell her that?

Claire (*apologetically*) I didn't mean to be taken so seriously.

Sadie You said there was a link between us — about something in the past.

Claire I don't really believe that. There's nothing particularly odd in my past.

Lloyd What about your twin sister and your husband disappearing off the face of the earth?

Claire I have neither a twin nor a husband.

Lloyd Well, you took me in!

Claire I meant to. That's all part of being a spy, isn't it? Spies don't tell the truth, do they?

Lloyd I'm afraid, Sadie, you've just lost your place as head of the class.

Sadie Have I?

Lloyd Of course, the lovely Claire has taken us all in!

Claire You were telling the truth, I suppose?

Lloyd Some of it.

Claire Clarify please!

Lloyd I did have a wife but she didn't disappear so much as cleared off with someone else. No mystery there!

Sadie Oh, you're trying to take me in, now, both of you. You're pretending not to have a secret! Well, you won't succeed. I know we all have a secret. I'm not the only one. Steve had a dark secret. He told me his wife jumped out of the window.

Lloyd What?

Sadie It was a bungalow, but still she had to have psychiatric help afterwards, that's what he said.

Claire That's unfortunate but I don't know if it qualifies for a dark secret.

Sadie Daphne had a secret too. I know she did. I heard her crying in the next room last night. Did you know she wrote poetry?

Claire What has that to do with anything?

Sadie It just proves what a deep person she is. Steve said so. He said she isn't the sort of person who would leave without saying goodbye.

Claire How should he know?

Lloyd I'm telling you, Sadie, you are completely on the wrong track.

Sadie Listen to mine then. Do you want to hear it, my secret?

Lloyd No, keep it to yourself. A secret is only a secret until you tell someone else.

Sadie But I have got a secret — something dreadful in my past. I must tell you.

Lloyd (*with a sigh; exchanging glances with Claire*) Go on then, unburden yourself. (*He sits in the armchair* R)

Sadie Thank you. It's on my conscience a bit — although he did deserve it. (*Pause*) It's about my husband. (*She moves* C)

Claire You told me — he left you. (*She sits on the settee*)

Sadie I didn't tell you all of it. He did leave me — but not exactly voluntarily.

Claire What do you mean?

Sadie He wasn't a very nice man, my husband. He was a butcher.

Lloyd I know a lot of nice butchers.

Sadie My husband wasn't a nice butcher. He worked in a big company shop and he'd often bring meat home he'd stolen, bits and pieces, wrapped up in his pockets. But sometimes he went further than that and stole a whole carcass.

Claire A carcass?

Sadie That's right. He did a deal with one of the men who delivered the meat. He dropped it off at our house and charged the company.

Claire Heavens! You mean your husband stole it!

Sadie I told you he wasn't a nice man.

Lloyd (*bored*) Is this your "secret"?

Sadie No, I'm just going to tell you. It was when they dropped off a pig, the last time. We'd gradually cleared the freezer so that he had room for it and then my husband set to work in the kitchen, jointing it. He was very good at it, very skilful. He put a lot of energy into it. I had to help him. I had to wrap the joints up in cling film for the freezer. I was his assistant. But that night he was in a bad mood and he kept shouting at me. "Get a move on! Look what you're doing! You're so clumsy!" He swore at me too, using bad words, and I don't like that. (*Pause*) So that's when I stabbed him.

Claire (*aghast*) You stabbed him!

Sadie (*quite matter of factly*) Yes, I picked up the carving knife and stabbed him in the neck. I didn't really mean to hurt him. I just wanted to shut him up!

Lloyd Is this the truth?

Sadie Of course. I stabbed him in the neck — just about here. (*She indicates where on Lloyd*)

Lloyd backs away looking uncomfortable

(*Not noticing his alarm; quite calm*) He looked at me with such a strange look on his face — amazement, I suppose that's what it was.

Lloyd I'm not surprised!

Sadie Yes, he was amazed but he didn't seem to have much pain. He just kept staring at me, flabbergasted he was. He didn't even swear. He fell down on the floor and began to choke. Then he lost consciousness.

Claire What did you do? Ring for an ambulance?

Sadie No. All I could think about was the mess he was making on the kitchen floor.

Claire This is terrible!

Lloyd It's incredible!

Sadie (*as if they haven't spoken*) The terrible mess on the kitchen floor, and I'd only just cleaned it too. I couldn't leave him there, bleeding all over the place, so I wrapped him in a sheet and pulled him across the room and down the cellar stairs. He was very heavy, a dead weight, but I managed it. I thought he groaned once or twice but he didn't open his eyes.

Claire You left him there — in the cellar?

Sadie No, of course not. I put him in the freezer.

Claire The freezer?

Sadie The freezer was in the cellar, he'd emptied it so he could put the pig in it. It was a chest freezer. So I put him in there. I tipped him in head first and the rest followed. He wasn't a big man. The worst bit was pulling the knife out.

Claire (*aghast*) You pulled the knife out!

Sadie I had to. It was my best one. He was still bleeding when I closed the lid of the freezer. I'm not sure if he was dead.

Lloyd Well, he's dead now!

Sadie The next problem was disposing of all that meat. I couldn't get it in the freezer.

Claire The meat?

Sadie Yes, the pig. A whole pig takes up a lot of room and the freezer was — well, full. I gave most of it away to the neighbours. I ate some myself. (*Thoughtfully*) I got awfully fed up with pork.

Claire This isn't really true — is it?

Sadie Yes, it is, but how do *they* know about it. That's what worries me.

Lloyd What makes you think they know?

Sadie Because of everything that's happened since, that's what. It's all a plot against *me*.

Claire You don't really believe that!

Sadie Yes, I do. It's obvious. Can't you see that?

Pause while Claire and Lloyd exchange puzzled glances

Lloyd (*sceptically*) Didn't anyone miss your husband?

Sadie No, nobody seemed to care. He was always falling out with people at work and threatening to leave. They just thought he'd cleared off. He hadn't any friends and no one in his family cared about him.

Claire Poor man!

Sadie It was his own fault. Nobody liked him. I told people he'd just walked out on me. I pretended to be broken-hearted, but I wasn't. The thing is though I was lonely. That's why I came on this thing, but I didn't know they'd find out. They must have known all along.

Lloyd Why do you think that?

Sadie That's why they asked me to come, just to trap me. I knew it, the Major and that foreign girl, the way they looked at me. I guessed they knew.

(*Looking unconcerned*) It doesn't matter. I can take it.

Lloyd and Claire exchange more puzzled glances

Steve enters through the french windows with Daphne

Lloyd (*exclaiming*) Daphne!
Claire Daphne!
Sadie Daphne, is it really you?
Daphne Don't make a fuss! Of course it's me!
Sadie (*going up to her*) I thought something had happened to you. I heard you crying last night, through the bedroom wall.
Daphne Oh, nonsense! I always make that noise. I can't help it. I suffer from adenoids.
Sadie Are you quite sure you're Daphne? You look like Daphne!
Daphne I am Daphne!
Sadie I'm just not sure.

Sadie, looking doubtful, slips out, exiting into the kitchen

Claire Are you all right? (*She crosses to Daphne*)
Daphne Of course, I'm all right. What is the fuss about?
Lloyd We thought you'd gone home.
Daphne That was what you were supposed to think,
Lloyd Do you want to explain?
Daphne Of course. They told me I should be the mole.
Claire You!
Daphne That's right! This morning. They approached me to be the mole. All I had to do was to stay hidden for a couple of days and then come out and say they'd been holding me prisoner. That way they thought I could convince you I was not the mole and you would all confide in me.
Lloyd What went wrong?
Daphne (*indicating Steve*) He came and found me.
Steve I'm sorry. I was absolutely sure you were being held against your will.
Daphne I was perfectly happy in that nice old barn over there. It has all the comforts of home and I didn't have to put up with silly chatter from anyone. I had peace and quiet and time to write some really good poetry. (*Glaring at Steve*) He spoiled it.
Steve Don't blame me! I was highly suspicious of their motives when I saw that taxi arrive back here. That's why I produced the gun. That gave them a shock.
Claire It gave us all a shock!
Lloyd Any more confessions from anyone? (*He looks at Claire*)

Claire We—ll, yes. They did suggest I might be the mole.

Lloyd Oh God!

Claire But I turned them down. What about you?

Lloyd (*innocently*) Me? (*Looking around*) Where's Sadie?

Claire She was here just now. I wonder if they asked her to be the mole as well.

Lloyd I wouldn't think so.

Steve What about you? Did they ask you?

Lloyd They didn't have to.

Claire What do you mean?

Dan enters c

Dan Now you've found Daphne I suppose I'll have to come clean! Come on in, Marie.

Marie enters, looking glum

Marie Hallo, all!

Steve Marie minus the accent.

Marie (*scowling at Dan*) I said it wouldn't work.

Dan You did very well, dear. It isn't your fault. So, ladies and gentlemen, I'm sorry it hasn't quite turned out as you expected, but we have got some good footage.

Steve Footage? Oh, you've been taping everything, I suppose.

Claire But Lloyd blocked the hole.

Dan Yes, he did, that one! (*He points left*) But there's anothere one — just there. (*He points to the top of the archway where there is a picture or ornament*) A very good vantage point.

Steve So what was the idea of it?

Dan I'm about to tell you. We're making a pilot for a television show. We thought instead of putting celebrities and other hoi polloi under pressure when they knew they were being recorded, we wanted to record the behaviour of ordinary people put under pressure who didn't know they were being recorded. Reality television at its best. We had your permission. You all signed the contract. It took us a while to find four people who would even sign the contract. Too many of them kept reading the small print. You didn't, or if you did, you didn't understand it

Steve I understood it perfectly. I told you I was treating it as a challenge.

Dan What about you others? Did you understand what we were doing?

Claire I thought I did.

Steve So there isn't any final show? There isn't any hundred grand either?

Dan Sorry — that was a bit of deception. The carrot to attract you, so to speak, but you can't hold us to it. It's in the small print.

Claire So why did you ask anyone to pretend to be the mole?

Dan To see who would crack first. We thought Daphne was the least likely to crack, so we isolated her. We wanted action, you see.

Lloyd You got rather more than you bargained for.

Dan Yes, I didn't expect the gun. (*Taking a gun out of his pocket*) Poor Marie had a fit when you pulled that.

Lloyd Her scream was distinctly un-Romanian, I thought.

Marie I did my best! I only came on this gig to be paid for it, I didn't know it was going to be life-threatening.

Lloyd Nor did we all!

Claire (*to Lloyd*) So what was your part in all this? You didn't see a hearse outside the window, did you? That was all part of the game.

Lloyd It was a sudden inspiration. I was covering up for the Major. There shouldn't have been a taxi outside either but he decided to take the night off. It looked a bit casual him going out for the evening when we all thought we were under surveillance.

Dan Sorry about that but I was a bit bored to tell you the truth so I went down to the pub. I didn't except anyone to notice. We'd put a little sedative in the coffee.

All except Lloyd look surprised

Sorry, but I didn't want you all snooping about on the first night. That didn't apply to Lloyd of course because he knew what was going on anyway.

Claire What do you mean — he knew what was going on?

Lloyd Isn't it obvious?

They all look at him

Guess!

Dan It was his idea! He couldn't get a job on TV, but here was one way he could shine. Celebrity status at last. He took you all in!

Steve What a cad!

Claire My sentiments exactly.

Lloyd (*to Claire*) It wasn't all play-acting.

Claire No?

Lloyd Anyway, it's over now

Claire Do we get paid anything?

Dan Why not? If we sell the programme you'll get paid, I assure you, quite handsomely too.

Steve I suppose that's some consolation.

Dan You took a chance, didn't you, that someone might really crack?

Lloyd More of a chance than we realized. (*Looking round*) Where is Sadie, by the way? She was here just now.

Daphne I hope you're not suggesting that Sadie would crack up?

Lloyd That's what I am suggesting.

Daphne That's nonsense! She's the most normal of the lot of you.

Sadie appears in kitchen doorway. She is hiding a kitchen knife behind her back

There she is!

Lloyd What have you got there, Sadie?

Sadie (*nonchalantly*) Nothing much!

Claire (*to Lloyd*) She has!

Lloyd (*going over to Sadie*) Come on, Sadie, don't be foolish!

Sadie (*backing away from Lloyd*) Go away!

Dan What's the matter with the silly woman. (*He goes over to Sadie*)

Sadie (*producing the knife from behind her back*) Keep away from me! I know your game!

Lloyd (*sharply*) Leave it to me, Dan!

Dan What is the silly woman talking about?

Sadie Don't threaten me!

Dan I'm not. (*Looking down at the gun and then waving it in the air*) This is ——

Before he can finish, Sadie lunges at him stabbing him in the chest. He falls back choking and gasping. He drops the gun

Marie (*giving a little scream*) Oh my God!

Daphne and Marie go to Dan's side. Lloyd picks up the gun

Claire (*gently*) Come and sit down, Sadie, over here.

Sadie goes with her tamely and sits on the armchair R

Lloyd Someone had better call the police.

Steve I will. There's a phone in his study.

Steve exits through the arch

Lloyd (*calling after him*) Call for an ambulance, too.

Steve (*off*) What? Oh, an ambulance — yes!

Daphne (*by Dan's side*) I think it's too late for that. (*She has blood on her*

hands)
Marie (*sobbing*) Oh no!
Lloyd (*going over, feeling for a pulse in Dan's neck*) You're right. He's dead.

They all look at Sadie

Sadie It's not my fault. It was self-defence. He was going to shoot me.
Lloyd The gun wasn't loaded.
Sadie I didn't know that, did I?
Lloyd I think you did.
Sadie Prove it.
Lloyd What about the contents of your freezer? That should interest the
    police.
Sadie I don't care! You all think I'm so stupid. Perhaps I'm more clever than
    any of you. Look at me! (*She stands up proudly*)

The Lights dim gradually, the others shrink back. A spotlight remains on Sadie

I shall be a real celebrity now! People won't ignore me any more. I shall be
somebody! People will notice me! I'll be on television. They'll write about
me in the papers and I'll publish my memoirs. (*Taking a step forward*) I shall
be a star!

CURTAIN

FURNITURE AND PROPERTY LIST

ACT I

SCENE 1

On stage: Table with two upright chairs. *On it:* selection of board games
               (including Monopoly and Scrabble)
             Three upright chairs
             Small table *On it:* plant pot
             Armchair
             Settee
             Picture of a country scene with horses, with a spyhole in it
             Standard lamp
             Broadsheet newspaper

Off stage: Small notice on cardboard (**Marie**)

Personal: **Steve:** spectacles
             Claire: handbag. *In it:* cigarettes
             Lloyd: mobile phone, watch

SCENE 2

Off stage: Tray *On it:* five cups of coffee, sugar bowl and milk (**Marie**)
             Handbag (**Sadie**)
             Magazine, handbag. *It it:* little book of poetry (**Daphne**)

SCENE 3

Off stage: Torch (**Lloyd**)
             Torch (**Claire**)

ACT II

Off stage: Glass of water (**Claire**)
             Kitchen knife (**Sadie**)

Personal: **Dan:** gun in pocket

LIGHTING PLOT

Practical fittings: Standard lamp
Interior: The same throughout

ACT I, SCENE 1

To open: Late afternoon, summer; daylight through the french windows

Cue 1	**Dan:** "One of you is a mole!"	(Page 12)
	Black-out	

ACT I, SCENE 2

To open: Evening, standard lamp on, general warm lighting, dark outside french
windows

Cue 2	**Daphne** goes across to **Steve** and sits next to him	(Page 16)
	Lights dim on R *and spot lights up on Daphne and Steve on settee* L	
Cue 3	**Lloyd:** "That's it! I'm out! I've won!"	(Page 18)
	Full lights come up on R	
Cue 4	**Daphne:** "Yes, quite!"	(Page 18)
	Lights fade on L *and spot lights on* R	
Cue 5	**Claire:** "OK"	(Page 20)
	Full lights come up	
Cue 6	**Dan** goes over and switches off standard lamp	(Page 21)
	Standard lamp off	
Cue 7	**Dan** turns off the light by the door	(Page 22)
	Black-out	

ACT I, SCENE 3

To open: Dim lighting, night time, curtains are drawn at window

Cue 8	**Lloyd** pulls back the curtains	(Page 23)
	Moonlight floods in	

Cue 9	**Claire** and **Lloyd** turn off their torches	(Page 23)
	Dim spotlight on them on settee	
Cue 10	**Claire:** "What can it mean?"	(Page 26)
	Black-out	

ACT II

To open: Daylight, general warm lighting, sun outside french windows

Cue 11	**Sadie:** "...than any of you. Look at me!"	(Page 52)
	Lights dim, spotlight remains on Sadie	
Cue 12	**Sadie:** "I shall be a star!"	(Page 52)
	Black-out	

EFFECTS PLOT

ACT I

Cue 1   **Lloyd:** "That's what we have to find out."   (Page 26)
                 Car door slams

ACT II

Cue 2   **Sadie:** "Isn't there?"   (Page 39)
                 Gun shot

FIREARMS AND OTHER WEAPONS USED IN THEATRE PRODUCTIONS

With regards to the rules and regulations of firearms and other weapons used in theatre productions, we recommend that you read the Entertainment Information Sheet No. 20 (Health and Safety Executive).

This information sheet is one of a series produced in consultation with the Joint Advisory Committee for Broadcasting and the Performing Arts. It gives guidance on the management of weapons that are part of a production, including firearms, replicas and deactivated weapons.

This sheet may be downloaded from: www.hse.gov.uk. Alternatively, you can contact HSE Books, P O Box 1999, Sudbury, Suffolk, CO10 2WA Tel: 01787 881165 Fax: 01787 313995.

Lightning Source UK Ltd.
Milton Keynes UK
UKHW020733221119
353993UK00007B/512/P

9 780573 114243